MASTERING BIBLE STUDY SKILLS

Paul Pyle

Student Worktext

purposeful design
p u b l i c a t i o n s
A Division of ACSI

LEVEL 1
GRADES 7 & 8

LEVEL 2
GRADES 9 & 10

LEVEL 3
GRADES 11 & 12

purposeful design.
publications
A Division of ACSI

Books, Textbooks, and Educational Resources
for Christian Educators and Schools Worldwide

Purposeful Design Publications is the publishing group of the Association of Christian Schools International (ACSI). We are committed to the ministry of Christian school education, to enable Christian educators and schools worldwide to effectively prepare students for life. As the publisher of books, textbooks, and other educational resources, Purposeful Design Publications strives to produce biblically sound materials that reflect Christian scholarship and stewardship, and that address the identified needs of Christian schools around the world.

Mastering Bible Study Skills–Student

Printed in the United States of America

ISBN 1-58331-128-9   Catalog #7062

Purposeful Design Publications
A Division of ACSI
PO Box 35097 • Colorado Springs, CO 80935-3509
www.acsi.org

Mastering the Bible

Do you want to read the Bible through?

Leave 80 hours for it. Plot out that time.

If we are going to know the Bible, we must adjust our lives to make time. Otherwise, we will never come into a worthy knowledge of the Word, for it is impossible to get from others the personal knowledge of the Word that is possible and indeed needful.

✔ You have mastered a book of the Bible when you can:

- Summarize the _____ of the book.

- Cite the _____ for each key passage.

- Identify the _____ of each chapter.

✔ To master the Bible in your lifetime, you should:

- Use _____ for everything.

- Study the Bible _____.

- Make time for _____.

- Memorize _____.

Verse Study Format

Text

Carefully read the verse or passage being studied. Copy it down the left side of the page. Use a translation recommended by your teacher or one you are familiar with.

_____

_____

_____

_____

_____

_____

_____

_____

_____

_____

_____

_____

_____

_____

_____

_____

Observation

Look for:
- ✔ contrast
- ✔ comparison
- ✔ repetition
- ✔ cause-effect
- ✔ figures of speech
- ✔ illustration of a principle
- ✔ summary or conclusion
- ✔ any other significant observations

Interpretation

Rephrase the passage in your own words. This is not a summary. The paraphrase should be at least as long as the original text. The paraphrase should simplify and expand on the ideas contained in the original text, perhaps using lively, contemporary language. Most important, the paraphrase should reveal careful thought and deep understanding of the passage. In this part of the verse study, you as the student will be doing interpretation.

Application

The application can be as short as a single statement or as long as a paragraph, but it should address the question, _So what?_ In other words, what difference can the truth of this passage make in my life? For many passages, the application can take the form of a rhetorical question.

Name

Verse Study Sample 1.3

Text

Psalm 1:1–2

Blessed is the man who walks not in the
counsel of the ungodly, nor stands in the
path of sinners, nor sits in the seat of
the scornful; but his delight is in the law
of the Lord, and in His law he meditates
day and night.

Observation

- contrasts blessed man's way
  with sinner's way
- "walks," "stands," and "sits," meaning
  he doesn't hang around with sinners
- doesn't just read God's Word;
  meditates on it day and night

Interpretation

The man who has it all together is not the
simpleton who listens to ungodly counsel,
or the fool who makes sin his habit, or the
cynic who mocks everything good and
wholesome. Rather, the man who has it all
together has such a passion for God's
Word that he can scarcely stop thinking
about it day and night.

Application

Do I really love God's Word, or do I take
in only what is necessary to get by?

Name

Journaling 1.4

Many Christians have found great benefit in keeping a journal record of the time they spend in the Scriptures. This ongoing project will help you improve your Bible study skills.

Format

You may keep your journal in any sort of notebook: spiral bound, composition book, three-ring folder or binder, blank journal book—whatever you prefer or your teacher recommends. But you should try to use the same notebook consistently.

The following three-step **Journal Entry Method** will help you get to know the Bible. Each journal entry should include at least one sentence for each of the three parts:

1 Observation

What does it say?
Identify the main event or idea in the passage.

2 Interpretation

What does it mean?
Identify one or more timeless principles the passage suggests about God, yourself, right and wrong, etc.

3 Application

What does it mean to me? How can I apply it to my life?
What would it mean if you were to make that principle a reality in your own life? Answer one of these questions:
- What values would take on increased importance?
- What current priorities would diminish in importance?
- How would I respond to people differently?
- How would I spend my time differently?

The key to making this a valuable experience is not quantity of words but quality of thought. You can increase the benefit of this exercise by spending at least as much time thinking and praying as you do writing.

Frequency

The object of this discipline is not perfection but consistency. You are encouraged to keep a journal every day; however, the minimum requirement for this course is five entries per week.

One final note—plan to spend most (if not all) the semester in one of the New Testament Epistles—any Epistle of 4 to 6 chapters *except 1 Peter,* which will serve as your "lab" for practicing your new skills. For variety, you may want to take brief excursions into other books of the Bible, but you should spend most of your time in your chosen book. You will soon find that you'll grow to enjoy and appreciate the passages more as they become a part of your life.

Notes

_____

_____

_____

_____

_____

_____

_____

_____

_____

_____

Effective Quiet Time

Practicing the Basics

a quiet place • enough time • the Word • prayer

A Quiet Place

• _____ with God.

• no _____

• no _____

• _____ (essential)

Enough Time
How much time is enough? Time to

• quiet _____

• meditate _____

_____

• pray _____

Morning or evening? It depends on

• your _____
  (morning person or evening person?)

• your _____
  (the time of day you usually have free)

Give God the best time you can!

The Word
Three-Step Journal Entry Method

1 _____

What does the text _____?

2 _____

What does the text _____?

3 _____

What does the text _____?

How can I _____ it in my life?

Read expectantly. Look for God's message to you for today:

• a command to _____

• a promise to _____

• a reason to _____

• a reason to _____

Prayer

• Pray _____

Respond to what you have just read.

• Remember, you are talking _____

Thank Him for His help and protection. Ask Him for the specific help you need that day, such as wisdom, patience, or stamina.

Name

Effective Quiet Time

Overcoming Obstacles

✔ _____

• Get rid of _____

• Keep a notepad handy to write down things you need to remember.

✔ _____

• _____

Any discipline grows more enjoyable with increased expertise.

• _____

Take a walk and talk with God.
If weather and circumstances permit, have your quiet time outside.
Read an extended passage aloud.
Pray aloud through a passage: read a verse or two and respond to God concerning what you read.

Other ideas (suggested by you or your classmates):

_____

_____

_____

Remember why you're here. Your time with God is primarily for His benefit, not yours.
The time you set aside to spend with God is a sacrifice for Him, because you love Him.

✔ _____

• If you meet God in the morning, set out everything you need the night before.
• Make a covenant with God that you will set aside time for Him every day for the next month.
  (But don't make promises to God you don't fully intend to keep.)

✔ _____

• Get more sleep. Whatever is keeping you up is robbing you and God of precious time together.
• Get less comfortable. Don't try to meet God in your bed. It's rude to fall asleep during a conversation.
• Read and/or pray aloud.

Introduction to the English Bible

Types of Bibles

1 _____ Bible

- includes biblical _____ ,

  perhaps with some _____ in back

- produced for _____ distribution

2 _____ Bible
includes features such as a
- cross-reference column

- _____

3 _____ Bible
includes reference Bible features plus

- book_____

- explanatory _____

- charts, graphs, and other extras

Text of the English Bible

1 _____
- not originally included
- inserted by medieval copyists or scribes

2 _____
- inserted after invention of printing press

3 _____
- indicated by
  ¶ symbol
  indention
  verse number in **boldface**
  ALL CAPS for first words

4 _italicized_ words are _____
words, not included in the original language but
needed to make sense in English

Margins of the English Bible

1 **marginal readings used for**

- _____ variations (passages
  in which some of the ancient manuscripts read
  differently than others; see Romans 8:1)

- alternative _____
  (passages that might be translated differently;
  see Romans 3:25)

2 **cross-references**

- symbol _____

- uses:

  New Testament _____ of

  or _____ to an

  _____ passage

  or a similar _____

  developed in a _____ passage

- format:

  _____
  (usually center, sometimes side)

  and/or _____

Name

Introduction to the English Bible

References to God

1 God (Hebrew *El*)

uses of *El*:

- to indicate _____
  (e.g., Genesis 1:1)

- to indicate _____
  (e.g., Genesis 35:2)

- to indicate _____
  (e.g., Psalm 8:5)

2 Lord (Hebrew *Adonai*)

meaning _____, _____

uses of *Adonai*:

- to indicate _____

- to indicate _____ authority

3 LORD (Hebrew *Yahweh/Jehovah*)

- unique: the only self-given _____
  for God (the others are more accurately
  considered titles)

- see _____
  where both *Lord* and LORD appear in the same
  verse; cf. Matthew 22:41–45, where Jesus uses
  that verse to stump His adversaries

Features in My Bible

- type of Bible _____

  _____

  _____

- study aids _____

  _____

  _____

- marginal reading format _____

  _____

  _____

- cross-reference format _____

  _____

  _____

- paragraph format _____

  _____

  _____

Name

Mastering Bible Study Skills 📖 *Student Worktext*

Study Guide

Mastering the Bible

You have mastered a book of the Bible when you can

- _____
- _____
  _____
- _____
  _____

To master the Bible in your lifetime, you should

- _____
- _____
- _____
- _____

Effective Quiet Time

Practice the Basics

1 _____

2 _____

3 _____

4 _____

✔ **A Quiet Place**

- _____
- _____
- _____
- _____

✔ **Enough Time**
How much time is enough?

- time to _____
- time to _____
- time to pray _____

Morning or evening? It depends on

- your _____
- your _____

Give God _____

✔ **The Word**
Follow the three-step Journal Entry Method

1 _____

What does the text _____?

2 _____

What does the text _____?

3 _____

What does the text _____?

How can I _____ in my life?

Read expectantly. Look for

- _____
- _____
- a reason to _____
- a reason to _____

✔ **Prayer**

- Pray _____
- Remember, you are talking _____

Study Guide 1.7b

Overcoming Obstacles

✔ _____

- Get rid of _____
- Keep a notepad handy to write down things you need to remember so you can refer to them later.

✔ _____

- _____

  Any discipline becomes more enjoyable with increased expertise.

- _____

  Take a walk and talk with God. If weather and circumstances permit, have your quiet time outside. Read an extended passage aloud. Pray aloud through a passage: read a passage and talk to God about it.

✔ _____

- If you meet God in the morning, set out everything you need

  _____

- Make a covenant with God that you will set aside time for Him every day for the next month. (But don't make promises to God you don't fully intend to keep.)

✔ _____

- Get more _____
  Whatever is keeping you up is robbing you and God of precious time together.

- Get less _____
  Don't try to meet God in your bed. It's rude to fall asleep during a conversation.

- Read and/or pray aloud.

The English Bible

Types

✔ _____

- includes biblical text, perhaps with some maps in the back
- inexpensive, for mass distribution

✔ _____

also includes features such as
- cross-reference column
- concordance

✔ _____

includes reference Bible features plus
- book introductions
- explanatory notes
- charts and graphs
- other extras

Text

✔ _____

- not originally included
- inserted by medieval copyists or scribes

✔ _____

- inserted after invention of printing press

✔ _____

- indicated by
  ¶ symbol
  indention
  verse number in **boldface**
  ALL CAPS for first words

✔ _____ words are printed in italics. They are words that were not included in

the original _____
but are needed to make sense in English.

Study Guide

Margins

✔ _____

uses:
- textual variations:
  passages in which some ancient manuscripts
  read differently than others

- alternative translations:
  passages that might be translated differently

✔ _____

     symbol: cf. (meaning "compare")

uses:
- New Testament quotation of or allusion to

_____ passage

- similar theme developed in a

_____ passage

format:

- _____

    (usually center, sometimes side)

and/or _____

References to God

✔ **God** (Hebrew *El*)

uses:

- to indicate _____
              (e.g., Genesis 1:1)

- to indicate _____
              (e.g., Genesis 35:2)

- to indicate _____
              (e.g., Psalm 8:5)

✔ **Lord** (Hebrew *Adonai*)

- meaning _____, _____

uses:

- to indicate _____

- to indicate _____ authority

✔ Lord (Hebrew *Yahweh/Jehovah*)

- unique: the only self-given _____
  for God. The others are more accurately
  considered titles.

- see _____,
  where both *Lord* and Lord appear in the same
  verse; compare to Matthew 22:41–45, where
  Jesus uses that verse to stump His adversaries.

Notes

_____

_____

_____

_____

_____

_____

_____

_____

_____

Name

God's Revelation to Humans

God has enabled humans to *discover* truth in different ways, including reason, investigation, and intuition. But in some of the most important issues—such as the meaning of life, the existence and nature of God, and life after death—we have no natural means of discovering truth. To enable us to find answers, God has made us dependent on Himself. In other words, we must look not to *investigation* but to *revelation*.

Research

Revelation is "the disclosure of something previously unknown." God has revealed truth to us in several ways. Look up the references listed in the left column to match them to the means of revelation on the right. (The number 2 indicates references for which two answers are correct. Give both.)

1. John 1:1, 14, 18

   _____

2. Exodus 10:1–2

   _____

3. Psalm 19 (2)

   _____

4. Numbers 12:6–8 (2)

   _____

5. Romans 2:14–15

   _____

6. Colossians 1:15

   _____

7. 2 Timothy 3:16

   _____

8. Hebrews 1:1–2 (2)

   _____

9. 2 Peter 1:19–21

   _____

a. Scripture

b. Christ
   (the Incarnation)

c. conscience

d. history/miracles

e. face-to-face
   (theophany)

f. nature

g. the prophets
   (including visions
   and dreams)

Reflection

Bible scholars divide the means of revelation into two categories:

- *general or unlimited*
  available to all people everywhere

- *specific or limited*
  available only to certain people at certain times

Which two means of revelation listed are in the *general* category?

_____

Some people argue that, since nature is a means of divine revelation, all that is necessary for salvation is that someone observe the wonders of nature and believe in the existence of the Creator. The apostle Paul knew that salvation could not come through natural revelation alone.

According to Romans 1:18–20, what effect does God's revelation through nature have on humans?

_____

_____

_____

According to Romans 10:9–14, what sort of revelation is necessary for salvation?

_____

_____

Name

Inspiration of Scripture 2.2

What the Bible Says About Itself

Use your Bible to match each statement below to the appropriate reference. (Some passages are used more than once.)

John 10:35 • 2 Timothy 3:16 • 2 Peter 1:19–21 • Matthew 5:18

_____ 1. Every part of the Scripture is inspired.

_____ 2. The Scripture is absolutely reliable; it cannot be broken.

_____ 3. Every part of the Scripture is useful for sound teaching.

_____ 4. The prophetic word did not come about by the will of man.

_____ 5. rather, as the prophet wrote Scripture, he was "moved" by the Holy Spirit.

_____ 6. The Scripture is useful for reproving wrong behavior and correcting wrong teaching.

_____ 7. The Scripture is like a light shining in a dark place.

_____ 8. The truth of Scripture is eternal; it will last longer than earth itself.

_____ 9. The Scripture is given by inspiration of God, which is another way of saying that it is the Word of God.

What We Mean by Inspiration

Theologians use various terms to describe the inspiration of Scripture. Match the terms below with their meanings. (A couple of the terms in this section may be unfamiliar. If so, you may be able to figure out what the matches are by the process of elimination. In any case, your teacher will review this section with the class.)

a. verbal inspiration
b. inerrancy
c. infallibility
d. plenary inspiration

_____ 1. The Scripture cannot fail.

_____ 2. The Scripture is without error.

_____ 3. The very words of Scripture were inspired.

_____ 4. All of the Scripture is inspired by God.

The Writing and Canon of Scripture

Scripture

Canon: list of _____ accepted as _____

Bible: _____ Book— _____ canons

Old Testament

✔ written in the _____ language

✔ last book written was _____ (c. _____ B.C.)

New Testament

✔ written in the _____ language

✔ last book written was _____ (c. A.D. _____)

How canons were finalized

✔ Tests used to recognize inspired writings:

• Is it _____ ?

Was it written by a _____ or an _____?

Do the people of God _____ to its authority by

_____ their lives according to its teachings?

• Is it _____ ?

Is it free of _____ in geography, history, etc.?

• Has it been _____ ?

Have believers throughout the church _____ it as inspired?

Has it been recognized for a _____ ?

Name

The Writing and Canon of Scripture

Old Testament canon

- motivations for establishing the Hebrew canon (end of first century A.D.):

  fall of _____

  _____ people scattered throughout the Roman Empire

  _____ ritual ceased

  _____ of Jews increased

  need to know which writings are considered _____ and to protect them at all costs

  rise of _____ :

  no longer considered just a minor Jewish _____ but now a major

  _____ religious force

  need to _____ Jewish writings from Christian writings

- timing: Jewish canon established by the end of the _____ century

New Testament canon

- primary motivation for establishing Christian (New Testament) canon:

  emergence of heretical groups publishing their own _____ ,

  including writings _____ to their views

  and excluding writings that did not _____ them

- timing: canon established by the end of the _____ century

How the Bible Came to Us

Hebrew Scribal Tradition

✔ copying one _____ + _____ at a time

   • cross-outs: maximum of _____ per manuscript

✔ _____ characters in copy and source to make

   sure copy is _____

✔ _____ old manuscripts so that defaced letters couldn't be copied

✔ results:

   • availability of ancient manuscripts: _____ older than medieval European copies

   • accuracy of manuscripts: _____ because of great care in transmission of the text

✔ illustration: Dead Sea Scrolls, discovered in the 1940s, predated then-existing Old Testament manuscripts by hundreds of years—no deterioration of the text

Important Ancient Translations

✔ the Septuagint (c. _____ B.C.)

   • its name: from the legend of the seventy Alexandrian Jewish scholars who translated the Scriptures

   individually and came out with _____ translations

   • its significance:

   the first major translation of Scripture

   it rendered the Scripture in _____ , the international language of that day

   Old Testament quoted by New Testament writers (who wrote in Greek)

Name

How the Bible Came to Us

 3.1b

✔ the Vulgate (A.D. _____)

  • its name: meant " _____ " tongue, which was Latin

  • its translator: Jerome, a gifted Church scholar

  • its significance:
    first translation of the _____ Bible
    the Bible of the Church for 1,000 years

Early English Translations

✔ Wycliffe's Bible (_____)

  • part of Wycliffe's efforts to oppose _____ in the Church

  • translated from the Vulgate, which was in _____

✔ Tyndale's work (NT 1525)

  • first English Scriptures translated from the _____ languages

    finished the New Testament, the Pentateuch, and Jonah before he was _____

    by Church authorities, convicted of treason, strangled, and _____

  • contributions:

    sparked new _____ in the English Bible

    his excellent work was the _____ for the English Bibles that followed

    Tyndale's dying prayer: "Lord, open the king of England's eyes."

✔ explosion of English translations in answer to Tyndale's prayer

  • causes:

    rise of vernacular (_____) languages;

    decline of _____

    invention of the _____

    the Reformation in Germany and England

How the Bible Came to Us

- results:

_____ English translations of the Bible by the end of the sixteenth century

need for a _____ translation

King James Version (_____)

- profound impact on English-speaking culture

- predominant English Bible for more than _____ centuries

Modern English Bibles

✔ Revised Standard Version (1952)

www.bible-researcher.com/rsv.html

- attempt to provide a modern standard English translation
- criticized for _being free in its renderings_ "blurred some of the finer distinctions of the New Testament views of translators

✔ New American Standard Version (1971)

www.vecbs.org/society/bible.html

- most _controversial/rigrously_ "word for word" of popular translations

- conservative translation produced by conservative scholars

✔ New International Version (1978)

- whole new translation

- international team of evangelical scholars

- outsold King James within _____ years of publication

✔ New King James Version (1979)

- updates _____ and syntax of King James Version

- gaining in popularity

Name

Scribal Project

For this project, you will set up your own "lab" where you will conduct several field experiences over the course of this semester. Your assignment is to perform the function of a scribe and make a perfect copy of one of the New Testament Epistles.

Here are the details:

1 Choose a favorite New Testament Epistle (except 1 Peter) of 4 to 6 chapters.

2 Copy the text carefully and neatly in ink. No *cross-outs* are allowed. If you make a mistake, start that page over with a clean sheet.

3 Be sure to leave plenty of white space for notations and observations you will need to record later. Leave a space after each line, and use only the left half of the page (so that the entire right side is available for you to use as an extra-wide "margin").

4 To make it easier later on for you to move back and forth through this document, you should include reference information at the top of each page in the upper right-hand corner (e.g., James 3:2–3). Depending on the size of your handwriting, you'll get anywhere from two to five verses on a single page.

5 Bind the finished document in a folder. Label the front page with the name of the book you copied and your own name as "scribe."

6 As you work, you will probably notice things you had not noticed before in your reading or study of that book. Keep a pencil nearby to record your observations in the extra-wide margin.

Your work will be graded on three simple qualities: neatness, careful following of directions, and timely submission of the assignment.

Notes

Name

What's Different About a Paraphrase?

Just as an orange is a kind of fruit, so a paraphrase is a kind of translation.
But there are several important differences between a paraphrase and a standard translation:

Paraphrase

- _____
  more important than accuracy

- closer to _____

  for _____

- closer to _____
  word order

- uses familiar _____
  in place of unfamiliar ones

- usually the work of _____

- good for _____

  reading and easy _____

Translation

- _____
  and readability both important

- closer to _____

  for _____

- closer to _____
  word order

- usually lets unfamiliar word

  pictures _____

- usually the work of _____

- good for _____ ,

  _____ , and general use

Practice Translation Project

> Wherefore having girded up the loins of your mind being sober perfectly hope in the being
>
> brought to you grace at revelation of Jesus Christ as children of obedience not
>
> fashioning yourselves to the former in your ignorance desires but according as he who
>
> called you holy also yourselves holy in all conduct be you because it has been written
>
> "holy be you because I holy am"

The text shown above is a word-for-word rendering of a passage of Scripture. **Your task is to unravel the meaning of the paragraph and render it in standard English.** Remember that you will need to make several modifications to the text to achieve a good translation:

- You will need to break the text into sentences and add appropriate punctuation.

- You will need to rearrange the word order to fit modern speech patterns.

- You will need to supply words that are not necessary in the source language but are required in English (supplied words).

Even if you think you know where this passage can be found, you must resist the temptation to see how it is rendered in your Bible. You will gain maximum benefit from this project if you wrestle with the text on your own. As you concentrate on this passage, you will slowly see it come into focus, much the way a translator might see his work become clearer as he labors with the text.

Your grade will be based on the following:

- effort

- neatness of presentation

- quality of final "translation": correct meaning and smooth English style, neither word-for-word nor paraphrase

Submission requirements: Write your final "translation," along with all other information requested, on the "Presentation Page." Staple all revisions to the back of the "Presentation Page" so that the final version is on the front.

Name

Overview of the Bible Study Method

"What does it mean to me?" is an important question to ask in Bible study—perhaps the most important question—but it should certainly not be the first question. Careful students of the Bible take the time to work through three basic steps, answering three questions, to understand and apply the truth of the Scripture. You met these questions earlier, in unit 1, and answered them as you used the journal entry method in your quiet time. Now you will learn more about how to master a portion of the Bible by answering these questions:

The Three-Step Method:

1 Observation

What does the text _____ ?

2 Interpretation

What does the text _____ ?

3 Application

What does the text _____ ?

- How can I apply it to my life?

- In other words, what am I going to

  _____ about it?

The three steps in the journal entry method are actually part of our daily lives. Without thinking about it, we follow all three steps whenever we encounter:

- a traffic light

- musical notes

- a fire drill

Step 1: Astute Observation

Read the passage of Scripture with a discerning eye, looking for clues to the writer's intentions. Here are a few things that skilled interpreters are careful to notice:

✔ *Context:* the flow of thought

_____ the passage

- the _____ context:
  the verses before and after the passage

- the background and _____
  of the whole book; see Luke 1:1–4

- the _____ context:
  what was going on in the society of the writer
  and his audience

✔ *Genre:* the _____ of
literature, such as narrative, history, or poetry

✔ *Continuity:* _____ of
key terms or important topics

✔ *Proportion:* how much _____
is devoted to each topic (for example, how much
the Gospel writers gave to the last week before
the crucifixion)

Name

Overview of the Bible Study Method

✔ *Structural details:* the way ideas are

_____ in the passage

• rhetorical _____

• principle and illustration

• comparison and _____

✔ *Grammatical details*

• _____ reference

• _____ type

• phrases and clauses that _____
  words

✔ *Figures of speech:* Which ones did the writer use

and _____ ?

metaphor   anthropomorphism
simile   personification
hyperbole   euphemism
irony

Step 2: Balanced Interpretation

After carefully gathering all the data you can find in
the text, you as a skilled interpreter will articulate
the general principles underlying the text. To identify those principles, ask two important questions:

• What _____
  does the text address?

Biblical writers dealt not only with problems unique
to their times. They also addressed timeless issues
such as money, power, God, life after death, sex, and
family relationships.

• What light did the text shed on that issue for

its original _____ ?

Remember that in reading the Bible, you are looking
over someone's shoulder. The words on the page before you were originally intended for another person
or persons. You must be careful to discover what the
text would have meant to them in their circumstances before you try to apply those principles to
your own circumstances.

Step 3: Conscientious Application

Now that you have determined (as much as possible) the meaning for the original audience, you must
determine what that same text means in your own
life. Ask the following questions:

• What do I have _____
  with the original audience?

• What _____ did
  the writer seek from them?

• What am I going to _____
  about it?

This is the bottom line. All the work done so far is
futile if you fail at this point. The Scripture can have
no place in your life until it has an impact on your

_____ , the
choices you make in everyday life.

Name

Practicing the Bible Study Method

The passages listed below are familiar. However, you probably learned them as solitary nuggets of truth and never subjected them to the rigors of the inductive Bible study method. For each reference listed below, work your way through the three-step method. Examine the words closely (observation), identify general principles revealed (interpretation), and determine how the passage applies to you (application).

Philippians 4:13, NIV

Observation

What does the text say?

Some observations are given for Philippians 4:13 and its context. Others are possible. (*Remember that you won't find every observation detail in every passage.*)

- *Context*—What is the subject of the verses before and after verse 13?

   The subject of the paragraph is contentment in all circumstances. The writer, the apostle Paul, is in prison awaiting a trial that may end in his execution. In this passage, Paul is thanking the Philippians for their gifts, and he is telling them that he has learned to be contented whatever happens.

- *Genre*—What kind of text is this?

   Philippians is an epistle, or letter, to the Christian church at Philippi, which Paul began and now seeks to strengthen. Although Paul is in prison, he desires that the Philippian believers find patience and strength in Christ.

- *Continuity*—What key terms or topics are repeated here?

   Verse 13 is the last sentence in a paragraph that begins with verse 10. Words repeated are <u>concern(ed)</u>, <u>content(ed)</u>, and <u>I have learned</u>.

- *Proportion*—How much space is devoted to a certain topic?

   Chapter 4 is devoted entirely to personal messages of exhortation, thanks, and greeting to the Philippians. In this paragraph, vv. 10–13, Paul is answering the Philippians' concern by explaining that he has learned to be contented, and verse 13 tells how, "through Christ...."

- *Structural details*—How are ideas connected?

   Paul uses contrasts to emphasize his contentment: "I know what it is to be in need, and I know what it is to have plenty. I have learned the secret of being content ... whether well fed or hungry, whether living in plenty or in want." These contrasts strengthen the "everything" of v. 13.

Name

• *Grammatical details*—Is tense, use of modifiers, or another grammatical feature significant?

Modifiers: The phrase "through Him who gives me strength" modifies the main verb <u>do</u> in "I can <u>do</u> all things." Without the modifying phrase, Paul would seem to be boasting of his own ability, but he is giving all the credit to Christ.

• *Figures of speech*—What ones, if any, did the writer use and why?

"I can do everything" is an example of hyperbole, and Paul uses it in the way hyperbole is usually used, to emphasize his point. If he, a prisoner, can do everything even to the point of being content in prison, so can the Philippians, who have the same strong God, who, as Paul says in the next paragraph, "will meet all your needs."

Interpretation

What does the text mean?

• What timeless issue does the text address?

Contentment whatever the circumstances is an issue for all people of all times.

• What light did the text shed on that issue for its original audience?

If Paul could write from prison that he was content whatever the circumstances, then his audience, the believers in Philippi, could be content regardless of their circumstances. They too might have had to suffer for their faith, and they too could be strong in the Lord whatever happened.

Application

What does the text mean to me?

• What do I have in common with the original audience?

I have trouble being content with (my body, my family's income level, my abilities). [The students are not in prison, but some can name circumstances that threaten their contentment and cause them to seek the Lord's help.]

• What response did the writer seek from them?

That they should trust in Christ and thus be content regardless of the circumstances.

• What am I going to *do* about the truth of this passage?

[Here the students must make their own applications, but like Paul they need to look to the Lord for their strength in trials and not just try to muster up their own strength.]

Practicing the Bible Study Method

Jeremiah 33:3

Observation

What does the text say?

As you examine the following in Jeremiah 33:3, remember that not every observation detail will be present in every passage.

- *Context*—What is the subject of the verses before and after verse 3?

_____

_____

_____

_____

_____

- *Genre*—What kind of text is this?

_____

_____

_____

_____

_____

- *Continuity*—What key terms or topics are repeated here?

_____

_____

_____

_____

_____

- *Proportion*—How much space is devoted to a certain topic?

_____

_____

_____

_____

_____

- *Structural details*—How are ideas connected?

_____

_____

_____

_____

_____

_____

Name

Practicing the Bible Study Method

- *Grammatical details*—Is tense, use of modifiers, or another grammatical feature significant in the passage?

  _____

  _____

  _____

  _____

- *Figures of speech*—What ones, if any, did the writer use and why?

  _____

  _____

  _____

  _____

  _____

Interpretation

What does the text mean?

- What timeless issue does the text address?

  _____

  _____

  _____

- What light did the text shed on that issue for its original audience?

  _____

  _____

_____

_____

_____

Application

What does the text mean to me?

- What do I have in common with the original audience?

  _____

  _____

  _____

  _____

- What response did the writer seek from them?

  _____

  _____

  _____

  _____

- What am I going to do about the truth of this passage?

  _____

  _____

  _____

  _____

  _____

Name

Mastering Bible Study Skills Student Worktext

Practicing the Bible Study Method

2 Timothy 2:15

Observation

What does the text say?

(Remember that not every observation detail will be present in every passage.)

• *Context*—What is the subject of the verses before and after verse 15?

_____

_____

_____

_____

• *Genre*—What kind of text is this?

_____

_____

_____

• *Continuity*—What key terms or topics are repeated here?

_____

_____

_____

_____

• *Proportion*—How much space is devoted to a certain topic?

_____

_____

_____

_____

• *Structural details*—How are ideas connected?

_____

_____

_____

_____

• *Grammatical details*—Is tense, use of modifiers, or another grammatical feature significant in the passage?

_____

_____

_____

• *Figures of speech*—What ones, if any, did the writer use and why?

_____

_____

_____

_____

Name

Practicing the Bible Study Method

Interpretation

What does the text mean?

• What timeless issue does the text address?

_____

_____

_____

_____

_____

• What light did the text shed on that issue for its original audience?

_____

_____

_____

_____

Application

What does the text mean to me?

• What do I have in common with the original audience?

_____

_____

_____

_____

_____

• What response did the writer seek from them?

_____

_____

_____

_____

• What am I going to do about the truth of this passage?

_____

_____

_____

_____

_____

The Student, the Fish, and Agassiz

It was more than fifteen years ago that I entered the laboratory of Professor Agassiz and told him I had enrolled as a student of natural history. He asked me a few questions about my object in coming, and I replied that while I wished to be well grounded in all departments of zoology, I purposed to devote myself specifically to the study of insects.

"When do you wish to begin?" he asked.

"Now," I replied. This seemed to please him, and with an energetic "Very well!" he reached from a shelf a huge jar of specimens in yellow alcohol.

"Take this fish," he said, "and look at it. We call it a Haemulon. By and by I will ask you what you have seen."

With that he left me. Within ten minutes I had seen all that could be seen in that fish, and I started in search of the professor, who had, however, left the museum. When I returned, I resumed my steadfast gaze at my mute companion.

Half an hour passed, an hour, another hour. The fish began to look loathsome. I turned it over and around, looked at its face—ghastly; from behind,

beneath, above, sideways, at three-quarter's view—just as ghastly. I was in despair. At an early hour I concluded that lunch was necessary, so with infinite relief, I carefully replaced the fish in the jar, and for an hour I was free.

On my return I learned that Professor Agassiz had been at the museum, but he had gone and would not return for several hours. My fellow students were too busy to be disturbed by continual conversation. Slowly I drew forth that hideous fish, and with a feeling of desperation looked at it again. I was not permitted to use a magnifying glass; instruments of any kind were forbidden. My two hands, my two eyes, and the fish—it seemed a most limited field.

I pushed my fingers down its throat to see how sharp the teeth were. I began to count the scales in the different rows until I was convinced that such an exercise was nonsense. At last a happy thought struck me—I would draw the fish! And now with surprise I began to discover new features in the creature. Just then the professor returned.

"That is right," he said. "A pencil is one of the best eyes."

With these encouraging words he added, "Well, what is it like?"

He listened attentively to my brief rehearsal of the structure of the parts whose names were still unknown to me: the fringed gill—arches and movable operculum; the pores of the head, fleshy lips, lidless eyes; the spinous fin and forked tail; the compressed and arched body. When I had finished, he waited as if expecting more, and then with an air of disappointment, he said, "You have not looked very carefully."

"Why," he continued, more earnestly, "you have not even seen one of the most conspicuous features of the animal, which is as plainly before your eyes as the fish itself. Look again! Look again!" And he left me to my misery.

I was piqued. I was mortified. Still more of that wretched fish? But now I set myself to the task with a will and discovered one new thing after another,

The Student, the Fish, 7.1b
and Agassiz

until I saw how just the professor's criticism had been. The afternoon had passed quickly when, toward its close, the professor returned. He asked, "Do you see it yet?"

"No," I replied. "I am certain I do not, but I see how little I saw before."

"That is next best," he said earnestly, "but I won't hear you now. Put away your fish and go home. Perhaps you will be ready with a better answer in the morning. I will examine you before you look at the fish."

This was disconcerting. Not only must I think of my fish all night in preparation for my morning examination—studying, without the object before me, what this unknown but most visible feature might be—but also, without reviewing my discoveries, I must give an exact account of them the next day.

The cordial greeting from the professor the next morning was reassuring. Here was a man who seemed to be quite as anxious as I that I should see for myself what he saw.

"Do you perhaps mean," I ventured, "that the fish has symmetrical sides with paired organs?"

His thoroughly pleased exclamation—"Of course! Of course!"—repaid the wakeful hours of the previous night. After he had discoursed most happily and enthusiastically—as he always did—upon the importance of the point, I asked what I should do next.

"Oh, look at your fish!" he exclaimed, and he left me again to my own devices. In a little more than an hour, he returned and heard my new catalogue.

"That is good, that is good!" he repeated. "But that is not all; go on."

And so for three long days he placed that fish before my eyes, forbidding me to look at anything else or to use any artificial aid. "Look, look, look," was his constant injunction.

This was the best science lesson I ever had—a lesson whose influence has extended to the details of every subsequent study, a legacy of inestimable value that the professor has left to me, as to many others, one which we could not buy and with which we cannot part.

"Facts are stupid things," he would say, "until brought into connection with some general law."

At the end of eight months with Professor Agassiz, it was almost with reluctance that I left the study of fish and turned to my intended study of insects, but what I gained through this experience has been of greater value than years of later investigation in my favorite group.

Name

7.1b   *Mastering Bible Study Skills   Student Worktext*

*I*n this you greatly rejoice, though now for a little while, if need be, you have been grieved by various trials, that the genuineness of your faith, *being* much more precious than gold that perishes, though it is tested by fire, may be found to praise, honor, and glory at the revelation of Jesus Christ, whom having not seen you love. Though now you do not see *Him,* yet believing, you rejoice with joy inexpressible and full of glory, receiving the end of your faith—the salvation of *your* souls.

—1 Peter 1:6–9

Name

Peter writes his first epistle to believers who are facing grave suffering for their faith. He wants to remind them of who they are in Christ and what their salvation means. The twin themes of suffering (now) and salvation (yet to come) run like railroad tracks through the whole book. Almost every passage deals in some way with one or both of these key ideas.

For instance, the book opens with a salutation to "the pilgrims of the Dispersion . . . elect according to the foreknowledge of God" (1 Peter 1:1–2). Already, the two themes present themselves: from one point of view, Peter's audience is "elect," while from another point of view, they are only "pilgrims,"

not permanent residents. This is both good news and bad: his readers belong to God, but they do not belong to the present order of things. Peter's objective is to help them see which one of those two facts is more significant.

Your assignment is to do a topical study on these two themes in 1 Peter. Under each column shown below, list three words or phrases (along with references) pertaining to that theme for each chapter. If there are more than three such words or phrases, choose the best three examples from the chapter for presentation. The first chapter is done for you. Your assignment is to do the remaining four chapters from the book.

Chapter 1

Suffering

1   "grieved by various trials" (1:6)

2   faith like gold "tested by fire" (1:7)

3   "the time of your stay here in fear" (1:17)

Salvation

1   "hope through the resurrection of Jesus Christ from the dead" (1:3)

2   "receiving the end of your faith—the salvation of your souls" (1:9)

3   "grace that is to be brought to you at the revelation of Jesus Christ" (1:13)

Topical Study

Chapter 2

Suffering

1 _____

_____

_____

2 _____

_____

_____

3 _____

_____

_____

Salvation

1 _____

_____

_____

2 _____

_____

_____

3 _____

_____

_____

Chapter 3

Suffering

1 _____

_____

_____

2 _____

_____

_____

3 _____

_____

_____

Salvation

1 _____

_____

_____

2 _____

_____

_____

3 _____

_____

_____

Name

Mastering Bible Study Skills Student Worktext

Topical Study 8.1c

Chapter 4

Suffering

1 _____
_____
_____

2 _____
_____

3 _____
_____
_____

Salvation

1 _____
_____
_____

2 _____

3 _____
_____

Chapter 5

Suffering

1 _____
_____

2 _____
_____

3 _____
_____
_____

Salvation

1 _____
_____

2 _____
_____

3 _____
_____

You have completed a two-part topical study of 1 Peter. Your next assignment is to do a one-part topical study of the New Testament Epistle you chose.

Name

Literary Devices

Fill in the blanks in two phases. First, your instructor will help you fill in the blanks in the description of each literary device. Then you will do "Bible Study: Literary Devices" project to discover how each literary device is used in the biblical example.

Repetition

✔ Definition: A recurring word or phrase; it indicates

that the writer wants to _____
a point.

• Keys: _____

• Biblical example: _____

_____

_____

_____

Continuity

✔ Definition: This is like repetition, except it is an

_____ that is repeated, using different
terms. Like repetition, continuity serves to

_____ and sometimes to

_____ an idea.

• Keys: _____

• Biblical example: _____

_____

_____

_____

Cause-Effect

✔ Biblical writers often speak of one thing being
caused by another or of one thing being the

_____ of another. Often this device

appears in a _____ or in a

_____ . Biblical writers often use key
words that help us spot this device. The most

important key word is _____ ,
but cause-effect sometimes appears without any
of these terms.

• Keys: _____

_____

• Biblical example: _____

_____

_____

_____

_____

_____

Name

Literary Devices 9.1b

Comparison

✔ With this device, the biblical writer shows how

two things, ideas, or people are _____

• Keys: _____

• Biblical example: _____

_____

_____

_____

_____

_____

_____

Contrast

✔ With this device, the biblical writer shows how
two things, ideas, or people are different.

• Keys: _____

• Biblical example: _____

_____

_____

_____

_____

_____

_____

_____

Question

✔ This device takes two forms. In one form, the
writer asks a question and then answers it. In the
other form, called a rhetorical question, a writer
asks a question that has an obvious answer but
does not answer it. The purpose is to drive home
a point.

• Keys: _____

• Biblical example: _____

_____

_____

_____

_____

_____

Illustration

✔ With this device, the biblical writer uses an

_____ (a brief story), or refers
to an episode in a well-known story, to illustrate a
point. Sometimes the writer states the principle
before telling the story, and sometimes the story
comes first.

• Keys: _____

• Biblical example: _____

_____

_____

_____

_____

_____

Bible Study: Literary Devices

1 What two kinds of people does the psalmist contrast in Psalm 1?

_____

_____

2 In Romans 1:26 the effect was "God gave them up." What was the cause? Can you find the cause-effect in Romans 1:25?

_____

_____

_____

_____

3 What device does Paul use three times to open the sixth chapter of Romans? What similar example do you find in verse 15?

_____

_____

_____

Why does Paul use this literary device?

_____

_____

_____

4 What literary device does Paul use in Romans 7:1–6 to illustrate the believer's freedom from sin?

_____

_____

_____

_____

5 Peter discusses the believer's hope near the beginning of his first Epistle (1 Peter 1:3–12). What different expressions does he use to refer to the believer's hope?

verse 3: _____

verse 4: _____

_____

verse 5: _____

verse 7: _____

_____

verse 9: _____

_____

_____

What literary device is Peter using here?

_____

_____

_____

Name

Bible Study: Literary Devices

6 What does Paul contrast with the "works of the flesh" in Galatians 5:19–23?

_____

7 To what does the psalmist compare the godly man in Psalm 1?

_____

To what does he compare the ungodly man?

_____

_____

Are these literal comparisons or figurative comparisons?

_____

_____

What is the difference between figurative and literal comparisons?

_____

_____

_____

_____

_____

_____

_____

8 What expression does Jesus repeat to emphasize His point in Matthew 5:21–44?

_____

_____

9 Jesus often used literary devices. Read the parable in Mark 4:3–9 and its explanation in Mark 4:14–20. What comparisons and contrasts do you see?

_____

_____

_____

_____

_____

_____

_____

Name

The Box Diagram  10.1

The box diagram is a highly visual, simplified presentation of the flow and pattern of a passage of Scripture (a paragraph, a chapter, or even a book). Look at the first Psalm to find the missing words in the box diagram shown below:

Notice the essential parts of the diagram:

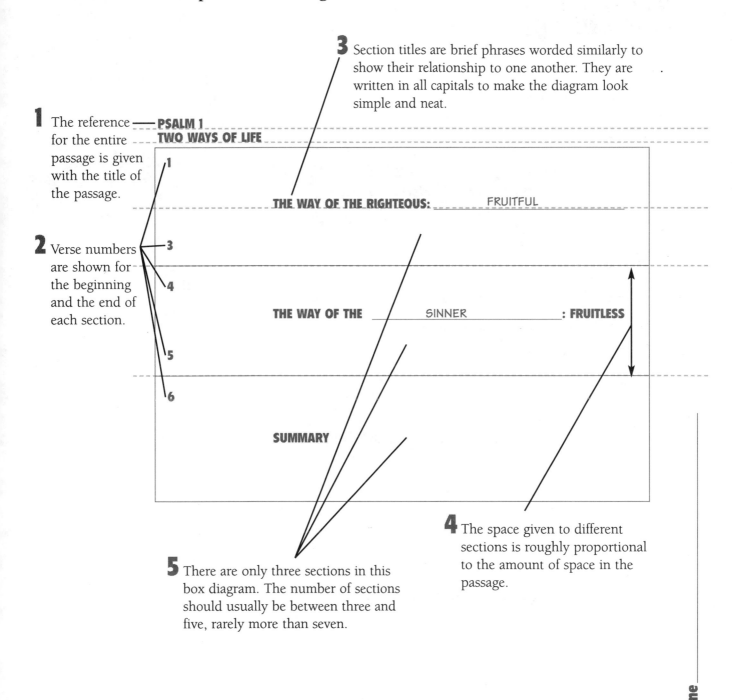

3 Section titles are brief phrases worded similarly to show their relationship to one another. They are written in all capitals to make the diagram look simple and neat.

1 The reference for the entire passage is given with the title of the passage.

2 Verse numbers are shown for the beginning and the end of each section.

PSALM 1
TWO WAYS OF LIFE

1

THE WAY OF THE RIGHTEOUS: FRUITFUL

3

4

THE WAY OF THE   SINNER   : FRUITLESS

5

6

SUMMARY

4 The space given to different sections is roughly proportional to the amount of space in the passage.

5 There are only three sections in this box diagram. The number of sections should usually be between three and five, rarely more than seven.

Name

Fill in the missing verse numbers in the box diagram of Psalm 73.
(Remember that the size of the section indicates its proportion in the passage.)

PSALM 73
A CHANGE IN PERSPECTIVE

1

ENVY OF THE WICKED

_____

TURNING POINT: UNDERSTANDING THEIR END

_____

_____

GRATITUDE TO GOD

28

Box Diagrams for 1 Peter 10.3a

Use the book of 1 Peter and the word bank for each diagram to fill in the blanks (words and verse numbers) under the section titles. This set of box diagrams is like the ones you will do for your "Topical Study" book.

1 Peter

A Change in Perspective

1:1

THE BELIEVER'S _____

2:3

2: _____

THE BELIEVER'S _____

3: _____

3:9

THE BELIEVER'S _____

4:19

5:1
5:14   FINAL INSTRUCTIONS

Word Bank

SUFFERING   RELATIONSHIPS   INHERITANCE

Mastering Bible Study Skills Student Worktext   10.3a

Box Diagrams for 1 Peter 10.3b

1 Peter 1:1–2:3

The Believer's Inheritance

1:1 **GREETINGS**	
1:2	

1:3

_____ **THROUGH SALVATION**

1: _____

1: _____

HOLINESS THROUGH _____

1: _____

1:22

_____ **THROUGH THE WORD**

2:3

Word Bank

HOPE	NEW BIRTH	REDEMPTION

Name

Box Diagrams for 1 Peter 10.3c

1 Peter 2:4–3:8

The Believer's Relationships

2:4

BELIEVERS TO CHRIST:_____ STONES AND _____

2:____

2:____

BELIEVERS TO _____: SUBMISSION

2:____

2:____

SERVANTS TO _____: SUBMISSION

2:____

3:____

WIVES TO _____: SUBMISSION

3:____

3:____

_____ TO WIVES: SENSITIVITY

3:____

ONE TO ANOTHER: _____

Word Bank

| CORNERSTONE | GOVERNMENT | LIVING |
| COURTESY | HUSBANDS | MASTERS |

Name

Box Diagrams for 1 Peter 10.3d

1 Peter 3:9–4:19

The Believer's Suffering

3:9

_____ IN SUFFERING

3: _____

3: _____ **CHRIST'S** _____ IN SUFFERING

3: _____

4: _____

THE BELIEVER'S _____ IN SUFFERING

4: _____

Word Bank

EXAMPLE	INTEGRITY	MIND-SET

Mastering Bible Study Skills 📖 *Student Worktext*

Box Diagrams for 1 Peter 10.3e

1 Peter 5:1–14

Final Instructions

5:1

_____ : SERVE AS _____

5: _____

5: _____

SAINTS: BE _____

5: _____

5: _____

BENEDICTION: BE _____ IN SUFFERING

5:14

Word Bank

SHEPHERDS   LEADERS   STEADFAST   WATCHFUL

Name

What the Bible Says About Interpretation

Proverbs 24:30–34

an illustration of observation and interpretation

Interpretation begins with observation. What did the writer observe about the lazy man's field?

_____

_____

_____

What conclusion did he draw from what he saw? (verses 33–34)

_____

1 Corinthians 2:14

requirement for understanding

Not just anyone can pick up a Bible and understand what God is saying. For some people the Bible is full of foolishness simply because they cannot understand what they are reading. What sort of person cannot comprehend spiritual things?

_____

_____

Deuteronomy 29:29

what we cannot know; what to do with what we know

When we come to a difficult passage of Scripture, we may want to know more than God really wants us to know. God has declared some matters "off limits" to our understanding. According to this verse, what things "belong to the Lord"?

_____

_____

Rather than trying to find out the "secret things," or the things God doesn't want us to know, we should invest our time and energy trying to understand the things God has revealed to us. According to this verse, why has God revealed to us what He has?

_____

_____

_____

_____

2 Timothy 2:15

what God wants from us when we're in the Word

What does God expect from those who handle the Scripture? He wants us to be

_____

2 Peter 3:16

a warning from Peter about careless interpretation

If you think some of the things you read in the Bible are hard to understand, you're in good company. Peter thought that some of Paul's writings were confusing and difficult. But that didn't mean that Peter thought it was all right to be careless about interpreting Scripture. What did Peter say about people who distort the Scripture?

_____

_____

_____

_____

Name

Biblical Interpretation 12.2

Two Principles of Interpretation

1 Scripture is _____ .

Therefore, it has _____ .

This means…
- We study the Scripture in order to know

  _____ and to

  _____ Him better.

- The Scripture has greater authority than

  _____

  (even religious tradition).

- The Scripture has greater authority than

  _____ .

  Therefore, it cannot _____ itself.

2 Modern readers are the _____ audience. Although Scripture was written for the benefit of all believers throughout history, it was originally written to meet particular needs at a particular time.

- Therefore, our first priority in studying Scripture is not to discover "what it means to me" but to understand what the text meant to its

  _____ or

  primary audience.

- Therefore, a passage has only one correct meaning, although it might have a wide variety of

  _____ .

  A single Scripture passage cannot have one meaning for one person and a

  _____

  meaning for another.

Two Features of Good Biblical Interpretation

1 Good biblical interpretation begins with

  _____ .

- Is it true that "money is the root of all evil"?

  See 1 Timothy 6:10. _____ .

- What *is* "the root of all evil"? _____

  _____ .

2 Good biblical interpretation uses

  _____ .

- We must interpret Scripture by

  _____ .

Always keep the _____

in view.

That is, be aware of the verses immediately

_____ the passage

and the teachings of the rest of

_____ .

- We must interpret Scripture _____ except when it speaks figuratively. Normally, we take the words of Scripture in their usual sense.

- We must be _____

  as we interpret Scripture.

Mastering Bible Study Skills 📖 *Student Worktext*

Interpreting Figures of Speech 13.1a

A figure of speech is a word or phrase used to communicate something other that its literal meaning. Figures of speech are used to enhance communication and to make writing more colorful. They should always be interpreted in context.

1 metaphor

a figurative _____

that uses a direct _____

• Example: "God is our _____ ."

  (Brainstorm other scriptural examples.)

• Interpreting metaphors: Decide what

_____ the two

things share. Why do you think the writer used figurative language instead of literal language?

_____

_____

_____

• What is the metaphor in Psalm 69:2?

_____

_____

_____

• What does it mean?

_____

_____

_____

2 simile

a figurative description using a comparison with

_____ or _____

• Examples: "[Man] comes forth like a flower… he flees like a shadow…." (Job 14:2)

• What are the two similes?

  "like a _____ "

  and "like a _____ "

• What do they both mean?

_____

_____

• Interpreting similes:

  Decide what important

_____

  the two things share.

• What are the similes in Job 7:1–2, and what do they mean?

_____

_____

_____

_____

Interpreting 13.1b
Figures of Speech

3 personification

speaking of a nonliving thing as if it were

_____

• Example: "Let the rivers clap their hands; let the
hills be joyful together" (Psalm 98:8).

• Interpreting personification: Remember that
personification is a figure of speech,

not to be taken _____ .

Personification _____
the writer's point.

• Find the example of personification in
Deuteronomy 32:1.

_____

_____

_____

_____

_____

_____

_____

_____

4 hyperbole

deliberate _____

for_____

• Example: "My tears have been my food day and
night" (Psalm 42:3).

• Interpreting hyperbole: Remember that hyperbole
is a figure of speech, not to be taken literally.

Its purpose is to _____
a point.

• Find the hyperbole in John 21:25, and explain
what it means:

_____

_____

_____

_____

_____

_____

_____

_____

Interpreting Figures of Speech

5 irony

saying the _____ of what is meant

- Example: "how glorious was the king of Israel today" (2 Samuel 6:20).

- Interpreting irony: Use the

_____ to determine how the words are probably intended.

- Find the irony in Job 12:2 and explain what the verse means.

_____

_____

_____

_____

_____

_____

_____

_____

_____

_____

_____

6 euphemism

substitution of a

_____ for one that might be unpleasant or offensive

- Example: He "did not know her till she had brought forth her firstborn Son" (Matthew 1:25).

- _____ a euphemism:

Use the _____ to determine what is actually meant.

- Write the euphemism in Acts 7:60, and explain what it actually means:

_____

_____

_____

_____

_____

_____

_____

_____

_____

_____

Interpreting Figures of Speech

7 anthropomorphism

speaking of God as though He possessed a

human _____

_____

•Example: "the eyes of the Lord" (2 Chronicles 16:9)

•Interpreting anthropomorphisms: Identify

what _____
of God is highlighted by the anthropomorphism.

•Find the anthropomorphisms in Psalm 10:1 and
10:11. Explain what they mean:

_____

_____

_____

_____

_____

_____

_____

_____

_____

_____

_____

_____

_____

_____

_____

_____

_____

_____

_____

_____

_____

_____

_____

_____

_____

_____

_____

_____

Name

More Practice with Figures of Speech

For each reference below, identify the figure of speech in that passage. Then match that reference to the interpretation statement. The first item is done for you as an example. (Notice how much more colorful the figures of speech are than the straightforward statements.)

metaphor   irony
simile   euphemism
personification   anthropomorphism
hyperbole

Interpretive Statements

_____irony_____ **Job 38:21** ○

_____ **Psalm 19:5** ○

_____ **Psalm 106:17** ○

_____ **Matthew 7:3** ○

_____ **Luke 11:39** ○

_____ **2 Corinthians 5:1–4** ○

_____ **James 1:15** ○

_____ **Job 9:25–26** ○

_____ **Psalm 19:1–2** ○

○ You make yourself look like a virtuous person when you really are morally and spiritually corrupt.

○ You are actually young and inexperienced, and you don't know what you are talking about.

○ Day and night reveal God's glory and show what He is like.

○ The sun shines brightly.

○ Job says his life is passing by swiftly.

○ Lust leads to sin, which leads to death.

○ We know that our corrupt earthly body will die, but we will receive an immortal heavenly body.

○ Dathan and Abiram were destroyed when God caused an earthquake, or similar event.

○ Why do you judge another person's smaller sin but fail to recognize your own, which is far greater?

Name

More Practice with Figures of Speech

For each reference below (all from 1 Peter) identify the figure of speech and explain what it means in its context. If you are not sure what it means, ask your teacher or your parents for help, or consult a commentary or another translation. The first is done as an example.

1:2 "sprinkling of the blood of Jesus" _____ *metaphor*

_____ *The death of Jesus pays for the sins of His people.*

1:13 "gird up the loins of your mind" _____

_____

1:19 "as of a lamb without blemish" _____

_____

1:24 "All flesh is as grass" _____

_____

2:1 "laying aside all malice" _____

_____

2:2 "as newborn babes, desire the pure milk of the word" _____

_____

_____

2:3 "you have tasted that the Lord is gracious" _____

_____

2:24 "the tree" _____

_____

2:25 "like sheep going astray" _____

_____

Name

More Practice with Figures of Speech

ow that you have identified figures of speech from the first two chapters, see if you can identify the figures of speech listed by reference only in the remaining chapters of the Epistle. For each reference listed below, write the phrase that contains the figure, the type of figure, and a brief explanation of its meaning in context. The first is done as an example.

3:12   "The eyes of the Lord are on the righteous, and His ears are open to their prayers;

but the face of the Lord is against those who do evil."

All three are anthropomorphisms.

The first two mean that God pays close attention to the needs of the righteous;

the last means that He opposes those who do evil.

4:1

5:2

5:5

5:6

5:8

(Note: Some figures of speech are still debated among Bible scholars. For instance, no one can be sure what Peter meant by the phrase "she who is in Babylon" in 5:13. Some interpreters think it is an early Christian code for "the church in Rome," while others think Peter was actually referring to a woman in Babylon, known to his audience, who sends her greetings.)

Name

The Creative Paraphrase 14.1

For this project, you will rewrite the text of selected chapters from your "Scribal Project" in a paraphrase aimed at a specific audience. You will serve as an "interpreter" between the message of the book you've been studying and your audience, who may not understand standard English well enough to get the message. Keep both ends of the bridge attached. In other words, don't identify so closely with your audience that you lose sight of the message you want to communicate, but don't think so much about the message that you forget your audience's needs.

✔**1 Identify a target audience,** a group of people for whom standard English might not communicate very well. (This should be a group whose jargon you can use effectively.)

Choose a group listed below or another whose dialect you know well. If you prefer, address your paraphrase to children, using short sentences and simple vocabulary.

surfers

rappers

cowboys

hippies

athletes

✔**2 Make sure you understand the chapters you selected** well enough to explain them simply and directly to someone else.

• Be careful not to use words or expressions your target audience would not readily understand.

• You may have to "translate" some figures of speech from the text to word pictures closer to the experiences of your audience.

Keep in mind that vocabulary, sentence complexity, and sentence length should be tailored to the needs and abilities of your audience.

✔**3 Write the source translation** (from a standard English Bible) down the left side of the page, allowing plenty of room on the right side for your paraphrase. (Since the paraphrase will probably take up more space than the original text, you should stop the source text about 2/3 to 3/4 down the page.)

✔**4 Write the paraphrase in pencil** on the right-hand side of the page. Using a pencil will make it easier for you to revise your work as you go.

✔**5 When you have finished your paraphrase, write an introduction** to your work explaining how the needs of your target audience are unusual enough to warrant a special paraphrase. Explain how your paraphrase addresses those special concerns.

Name

Bible Study Tools 15.1a

Study Bible

a reference Bible with study helps, including

_____

_____

_____

Concordance

an _____ listing of Bible words with

_____and _____

Bible Dictionary

_____ arranged _____

of Bible _____ and Bible _____

and other biblical _____

Parallel Text Bible

two or more versions of the Bible arranged _____

on the _____ for easy comparison

Bible Study Tools  15.1b

Commentary

_____ and _____

of the biblical text, written by Bible _____

Topical Bible

selection of _____ arranged

alphabetically according to _____

Word Study Bible

explanations of biblical terms in the _____

language: Hebrew in the Old Testament and _____

in the New Testament

Bible Atlas

_____ of Bible lands during Bible _____

The Right Tool for the Job 15.2

For each of the situations described below, identify the first tool you would consult. Also indicate which other tool(s) you might use as secondary sources.

Study Bible
Concordance
Bible Dictionary
Parallel Text Bible

Commentary
Topical Bible
Word Study Bible
Bible Atlas

1 What does 1 Peter 3:19–20 mean?

2 Where is that verse that says, "Many are called but few are chosen"?

3 Where can I find background information on the book of Titus?

4 What is the meaning of the verse that says, "Purge me with hyssop and I shall be clean"?

5 What does Isaiah 30:33 mean?

6 What are demons, and where did they come from?

7 What does the Bible have to say about alcoholic beverages?

8 What exactly is meant by the New Testament word *justified*?

9 Who was Amos?

10 Why was it significant that Jesus chose to travel through Samaria and that He talked with the Samaritan woman?

11 What does the New Testament say about sexual sin?

12 What does the word *fornication* actually mean? Is there one Greek word translated *fornication*, or are there several different terms translated by the same English word?

13 Where can I find information on the three Greek words translated *love*?

14 Why did Paul refuse to have Titus circumcised (Galatians 2:3)?

15 How does Psalm 23 differ in the King James Version and the New International Version?

Name

Interpreting a Difficult Passage

This project will help you learn to use the tools you just studied. To complete it, select a problem passage from your "Scribal Project" or from 1 Peter. (An example from 1 Peter is shown at the right.)

1 **Identify an interpretive problem.** Look for a difficult passage in your "Scribal Project" book, something that hasn't made sense to you as you've studied the book this semester, or a difficult passage in 1 Peter (other than the example).

2 **Find at least two different interpretations of the passage.** There will often be more than two interpretations of difficult passages, but you need to find only two.

3 **Take note of the evidence used to support the different views.** This might include key terms, cultural background, cross-references, etc.

4 **Select and defend the interpretation that seems most sound to you.**

5 Presentation:
- Copy or summarize the passage.
- Identify the interpretive problem.
- State each interpretation briefly.
- Identify the interpretation you think is most sound.
- Explain why you chose that interpretation.
- List all the reference tools you consulted, even those in which you found nothing helpful.

Remember that the passages you are dealing with have puzzled wise and godly men and women for centuries. No view is obviously right. As you state the interpretation you chose, defend it as strongly as you can without implying that it's the only interpretation possible.

Sample Study

The problem passage

1 Peter 3:19–20 says that Christ "preached to the spirits in prison, who formerly were disobedient . . . in the days of Noah. . . ."

The interpretive problem

Who were the "spirits," and how did Christ "preach" to them?

Two major interpretations

1. Jesus went to the place where the fallen angels are held and declared His final victory over them.

2. Christ "preached" through Noah to the wicked people of Noah's day.

The first view seems better

1. The word translated "spirits" usually referred to angels in ancient Christian writing, so the "spirits" were probably not humans.

2. The word translated "preached" is different from the word used for "proclaimed the gospel," so it probably doesn't refer to Noah's offering salvation to his neighbors.

Resources used

The *Nelson Study Bible*
The *Amplified Bible*
The *NIV Bible Commentary*
The *NIV Study Bible*
The *IVP Bible Background Commentary*

Name

Difficult Passage Project 15.4a

Name _____

Date _____ **Class/Period** _____

The problem passage: _____

_____

_____

_____

_____

The interpretive problem: _____

_____

_____

_____

_____

Two of the major interpretations: _____

1 _____

_____

_____

_____

2 _____

_____

_____

_____

_____

Difficult Passage Project 15.4b

Why the _____ **view seems better:**

1 _____

_____

_____

_____

2 _____

_____

_____

_____

Resources used: _____

_____

_____

_____

_____

Time I have spent on this project _____

Grade I deserve and why _____

Number of times I have read/studied the text for this project _____

So what? _____

_____

_____

_____

_____

Name _____

Applying Biblical Truth  16.1

Part One: A Miserable Ambition

No one plans to become proud, unstable, immature, and self-deceiving, yet that is the direction many Christians are headed, including many Christian school students. These are people who make the deadly mistake of assuming that knowing about the Bible is enough. It isn't. The Scriptures make it clear that it is not just foolish but dangerous to neglect applying to your life the truths you learn from the Bible. Look up the following passages to do the matching below.

a. Matthew 7:24–27 ○

○ **1** People who fail to apply what they learn from the Bible can never grow in their faith; they can never get beyond spiritual infancy.

b. 1 Corinthians 8:1 ○

○ **2** People who fail to apply what they learn from the Bible deceive themselves.

○ **3** People who fail to apply what they learn from the Bible become arrogant and proud.

c. Hebrews 5:11–14 ○

○ **4** People who fail to apply what they learn from the Bible are unstable when life gets rough.

d. James 1:22 ○

Part Two: Excuses, Excuses

A wise man once said, "An excuse is a lie stuffed into the skin of a reason." People who know what the Bible teaches have no excuse for failing to obey God's Word. But that doesn't stop many Christians from creating their own lame excuses. Use the lines below to do some brainstorming. What are your favorite excuses for not obeying God? (We've provided some all-time favorites to help you get started.)

1 _____peer pressure_____   **6** _____

2 ____procrastination____   **7** _____

3 _____lack of time_____   **8** _____

4 _____   **9** _____

5 _____   **10** _____

Name

Applying Commands 16.2a from 1 Peter

For each command listed below, evaluate your own life: Do you obey that command as a pattern of life? This doesn't mean that you are perfectly consistent in every instance but rather that your obedience has become a habitual part of your character, your ordinary life.

For each command that has become a part of your life in this way, put a check mark in the "Doing It" column. When you find one that you typically do not obey, put a check mark in that column. Then use the space below the command to write your excuse. When you finish, you will get an idea of how well you are applying the truth of this book to your everyday life; you'll also learn what your favorite excuses are.

The commands are listed along with the references for the first chapter. Beginning with the second chapter, only references are listed; you will have to provide the command. You may change or add words to make the command clearer.

Possible answers are given.

Reference	Command	Doing It	Not Doing It
1 Peter 1:13	Gird your minds for action.		
excuse			
1 Peter 1:13	Be sober (self-controlled).		
excuse			
1 Peter 1:15	Be holy.		
excuse			
1 Peter 1:17	Conduct yourselves in fear (with reverence).		
excuse			

Name

Applying Commands from 1 Peter

Reference	Command	Doing It	Not Doing It
1 Peter 1:22	Love one another fervently with a pure heart.		
excuse			
1 Peter 2:2			
excuse			
1 Peter 2:11			
excuse			
1 Peter 2:13			
excuse			
1 Peter 2:15			
excuse			
1 Peter 2:17			
excuse			

Name

Applying Commands from 1 Peter

Reference	Command	Doing It	Not Doing It
1 Peter 3:8			
excuse			
1 Peter 3:15			
excuse			
1 Peter 4:1			
excuse			
1 Peter 4:7			
excuse			
1 Peter 4:8			
excuse			
1 Peter 4:9			
excuse			

Name

Applying Commands 16.2d from 1 Peter

Reference	Command	Doing It	Not Doing It
1 Peter 4:10			
excuse			
1 Peter 4:13			
excuse			
1 Peter 5:5			
excuse			
1 Peter 5:6			
excuse			
1 Peter 5:8			
excuse			
1 Peter 5:9			
excuse			

Name

Applying Commands from

Name _____

Date _____ Class/Period _____

This project is modeled after the exercise you did in 1 Peter. This time, however, you must find the commands in your "Scribal Project" book. Follow the same format used in the previous exercise. You should find at least three commands for each chapter (more, if you can find them) and at least 10 for the entire book.

For each command that has become a part of your life in this way, put a check mark in the "Doing It" column. When you find one that you typically do not obey, use the space in the command column to write your excuse.

Reference	Command	Doing It	Not Doing It
excuse			
excuse			
excuse			
excuse			

Reference	Command	Doing It	Not Doing It
_____	_____		
_____	_____		
excuse _____	_____		
_____	_____		
_____	_____		
excuse _____	_____		
_____	_____		
_____	_____		
excuse _____	_____		
_____	_____		
_____	_____		
excuse _____	_____		
_____	_____		
_____	_____		
excuse _____	_____		
_____	_____		
_____	_____		
excuse _____	_____		

Grade I deserve _____ **Time I spent on this project** _____

So what? _____

Name _____

Personalizing Scripture 17.1

Your assignment is to "customize" passages of Scripture selected from 1 Peter or from your "Scribal Project" book by substituting your own name. Here is an example:

> Dan should be self-controlled and alert. His enemy the devil
>
> prowls around like a roaring lion looking for someone to devour.
>
> Dan must resist him, standing firm in the faith, because he knows
>
> that his brothers throughout the world are undergoing the same
>
> kind of sufferings. And the God of all grace, who called Dan to his
>
> eternal glory in Christ, after Dan has suffered a little while, will
>
> himself restore Dan and make him strong, firm, and steadfast.
>
> 1 Peter 5:8–10, NIV

This method of application will make the Scripture come alive for you as you picture yourself in the passage. (Notice that you don't always have to use your name. In some places a personal pronoun such as *he, she, him,* or *her* would work better.)

Your grade for this project will be based entirely on the number of verses you personalize, as shown on the chart below:

50 or more verses	**A**
40–49 verses	**B**
30–39 verses	**C**
20–29 verses	**D**
fewer than 20 verses	**F**

You may choose from the 1 Peter passages listed below, or you may use passages from your "Scribal Project" book, or a combination of the two. Rewrite the verses by hand (no word processors allowed), inserting your name and personal pronouns where appropriate.

1 Peter 1:3–9	**1 Peter 3:8–12**
1 Peter 1:13–21	**1 Peter 3:13–17**
1 Peter 1:22–2:3	**1 Peter 4:1–6**
1 Peter 2:4–12	**1 Peter 4:7–11**
1 Peter 2:13–24	**1 Peter 4:12–19**
1 Peter 3:1–7	**1 Peter 5:5–11**

The final step in this project is to read your work aloud to yourself. As you read, let these passages become prayers. You will find that there is great value in praying this personalized Scripture aloud. Find a quiet place where you can be alone, and voice these prayers to God. (Your instructor will ask whether you have completed this portion of the assignment.)

Name

Writing Scripture as Prayer 17.2

The problem is familiar, and it's been around since the beginning of Christianity: Sometimes we don't know exactly how we ought to pray for people we care for. The apostle Paul put it this way: "For we do not know what we should pray for as we ought" (Romans 8:26). What if you could pray for someone with great confidence that you were praying God's will? That's what you will do in this project. You will rewrite a passage of Scripture as a prayer for a friend or loved one.

It's a wonderful thing to be able to pray Scripture for someone you are concerned about. One man, whose daughter had become ill, wrote Scripture prayers for her from the Psalms and kept them in a journal. Those Scripture prayers were a great encouragement to him as he prayed for his daughter.

For this project, choose one or more loved ones you would like to bring before God in prayer. This project is similar to the one you just completed, except that this time you will apply the Scripture in intercessory prayer for a friend, a family member, or some other loved one. Choose prayers recorded in your "Scribal Project" book (there are several beautiful prayers in Paul's Epistles) or perhaps other passages of Scripture that can be rendered as prayers. An example is shown below:

> May Laura rid herself of all malice and all deceit, hypocrisy, envy, and slander of every kind. Like a newborn baby, may Laura crave pure spiritual milk, so that by it she may grow up in her salvation, now that she has tasted that the Lord is good.
>
> 1 Peter 2:1–3, NIV

Again, your grade will be based on the number of verses you personalize, as shown on the chart:

50 or more verses	**A**
40–49 verses	**B**
30–39 verses	**C**
20–29 verses	**D**
fewer than 20 verses	**F**

Unlike the previous project, however, you will select the passages yourself. In addition to 1 Peter and your "Scribal Project" book, you can use the Psalms and other prayers in the Bible. Whatever you use, be selective. Some passages are better suited to writing as prayer than others. Use your own paper to write your project.

Finally, get alone someplace and pray aloud for the person or people about whom you wrote these prayers.

Name

How to Apply Scripture 17.3

We face two kinds of *problems* in applying Scripture to our daily lives. One kind of problem is cultural; the other is personal.

✔**1** **The cultural problem:**
The Scripture was written in the ancient Near East. Naturally, it reflects some of the customs and ways of thinking of that era. How can we apply to our lives principles from a document written thousands of years ago?

✔**2** **The personal problem:**
Application takes serious _____. As difficult as it may be to make careful observations, it is even more difficult to do the hard work of thinking through the meaning of Scripture in our daily lives. It's much easier to file away all our biblical knowledge and keep it safely out of our lives.

_____ will fight us on this point. Our deadly enemy doesn't care how much Scripture we study, even how much we commit to memory, as long as we don't begin to mix it into our daily lives. Once we begin to think about how to apply God's Word to our values, relationships, work habits, and other aspects of daily life, Satan begins to resist our efforts.

There are two steps in the *process* of applying Scripture to our daily lives.

✔**1** **After reading the passage, ask yourself these questions about it:**

  a. Is there an _____ for me to follow?

  b. Is there _____ for me to avoid?

  c. Is there a _____ for me to claim?

  d. Is there a _____ . for me to repeat?

  e. Is there a _____ for me to obey?

  f. Is there an _____ for me to avoid?

✔**2** **After reading the passage, ask yourself these questions about your life:**
If I were to make this biblical truth a part of my life right now,

  a. What _____ would I change?

  b. What _____ habits would I cultivate?

  c. How would my _____ change?

  d. How would my _____ change?

  e. What would I _____ more?

  f. What would I value _____ ?

Why did God bring me to this _____ at this time in my life?

What _____ stand between me and complete obedience on this point?

Name

Devotional Project 18.1a
Phase One: Observation

This project will combine most of the skills you have developed during this course. You will do the work in three phases, one for each step in inductive Bible study.

Choose a favorite passage of at least ten verses from your "Topical Study" book, one that you enjoy and know well. Use that passage to complete the following:

What passage have you chosen for the project? _____

List at least ten careful observations based on the passage. For your presentation, you will select some of your best observations.

1 _____

  _____

  _____

2 _____

  _____

  _____

3 _____

  _____

  _____

4 _____

  _____

  _____

5 _____

  _____

  _____

6 _____

  _____

  _____

7 _____

  _____

  _____

8 _____

  _____

  _____

9 _____

  _____

  _____

10 _____

  _____

  _____

Name

Devotional Project 18.1b
Phase One: Observation

What is the topic of the passage? _____

Do a box diagram of the passage. You will reproduce this diagram in your presentation.

Name _____

Devotional Project 18.2

Phase Two: Interpretation

So far you have identified the topic of the passage, outlined the structure, and made several key observations. Now you will use your interpretive skills to tell what the passage means.

✔ 1. **Identify and interpret at least three figures of speech in the passage.** Name each kind of figure (hyperbole, metaphor, etc.), and tell what it means in the context of the passage.

1 _____

_____

2 _____

_____

3 _____

_____

✔ 2. **Write a paraphrase of the passage, answering the following questions.** If necessary, use a separate sheet of paper to complete your paraphrase.

1 What is one timeless issue the passage addresses? What problems or concerns do you (a modern reader) have in common with the original audience? Your paraphrase should clearly deal with one central issue.

2 What response was the writer seeking from his audience? Did he want to stimulate his readers to trust God more? To turn away from sin? To be grateful for what God had done for them? Your paraphrase should make clear what response the writer sought.

_____

_____

_____

_____

_____

_____

_____

_____

Devotional Project 18.3a

Phase Three: Application

You have done careful observation in the passage, and you have interpreted its meaning. Now "put shoe leather" to the passage by applying it.

Read through the passage again with the following questions in mind. Answer those that apply to your passage:

1 Is there an example for me to follow? _____

_____

_____

2 Is there sin for me to avoid? _____

_____

_____

3 Is there a promise for me to claim? _____

_____

_____

4 Is there a prayer for me to repeat? _____

_____

_____

5 Is there a command for me to obey? _____

_____

_____

6 Is there an error for me to avoid? _____

_____

_____

Name

Devotional Project 18.3b
Phase Three: Application

Now answer these questions: If I applied this biblical truth to my life right now,

1 What habits would I change? _____

_____

_____

2 What new habits would I form? _____

_____

_____

3 How would my attitudes change? _____

_____

_____

4 How would my priorities change? _____

_____

_____

5 What would I value more? _____

_____

_____

6 What would I value less? _____

_____

_____

7 Why did God bring me to this truth at this point in my life? _____

_____

8 What obstacles stand between me and complete obedience on this point? ____

_____

Name

Course Evaluation 18.4

Use the titles below to answer the questions that follow:

Inspiration and Revelation
How the Bible Came to Us
Topical Study
Translation Project
Box Diagram Project
Structures Project
Figures of Speech Project

Creative Paraphrase Project
Bible Study Tools
Difficult Passage Project
Personalizing Scripture Project
Scripture as Prayer Project
Final Project: Devotional

1 Which part or parts of the course were most enjoyable?

_____

_____

_____

_____

2 Which part or parts of the course were most difficult?

_____

_____

_____

_____

3 Were any parts too easy? If so, which?

_____

_____

_____

4 What are two of the most important things you learned in this course?

_____

_____

_____

_____

5 Were any parts too rushed? If so, which?

_____

_____

_____

_____

6 What other suggestions would you make to improve this course the next time it is taught?

_____

_____

_____

_____

(continue on another page, if needed)